This journal belongs to

_____

Started on _____

Completed _____

Let's get social!
@Publications_International
@PublicationsInternational
www.pilbooks.com

TABLE OF CONTENTS

Gratitude 4

Hope 28

Faith 52

Love 76

Guidance 100

Peace 124

Grace 142

GRATITUDE

Let the beauty of the Lord our God be upon us: and establish thou the work of our hands upon us; yea, the work of our hands establish thou it.

—Psalm 90:17

Creator God, I am grateful for the world of nature. How beautiful is the work of your hands! Help me remember to slow down and notice the little things. All too often, I rush through life and don't notice the blessings all around me. I am grateful for the little bits of beauty scattered through my day. Thank you, God, for creating so much beauty in the natural world.

MY THOUGHTS

_____

_____

_____

_____

_____

_____

_____

_____

_____

_____

_____

_____

_____

MY PRAYER REQUESTS

_____

_____

_____

_____

_____

_____

_____

_____

_____

_____

_____

_____

_____

I'M GRATEFUL FOR

_____

_____

_____

_____

_____

_____

_____

_____

_____

_____

_____

_____

Thankful Grateful Blessed

In every thing give thanks: for this is the will of God in Christ Jesus concerning you.
–1 Thessalonians 5:18

Dear God, forgive me for complaining. Help me to remember that every time I have a headache, someone I know may have a hidden heartache; every time I don't like the food, millions have nothing to eat; every time my paycheck seems small, many have no paycheck at all; every time I wish my loved ones were less demanding, some people have no one to love. When I look around at my everyday blessings, my complaints seem little. Teach me perspective, God, and to always give thanks.

MY THOUGHTS

MY PRAYER REQUESTS

_____

_____

_____

_____

_____

_____

_____

_____

_____

_____

_____

_____

_____

_____

I'M GRATEFUL FOR

_____

_____

_____

_____

_____

_____

_____

_____

_____

_____

_____

_____

GIVE thanks WITH a grateful HEART

I will make them and the places round about my hill a blessing; and I will cause the shower to come down in his season; there shall be showers of blessing.

—Ezekiel 34:26

Lord God, my heart overflows with gratitude for all the blessings you have sent into my life. I am cognizant of the fact that I am probably only aware of a small percentage of them, though. You are such a generous God; you shower me with such abundance. I am grateful for it all, Lord.

MY THOUGHTS

MY PRAYER REQUESTS

_____

_____

_____

_____

_____

_____

_____

_____

_____

_____

_____

_____

_____

I'M GRATEFUL FOR

_____

_____

_____

_____

_____

_____

_____

_____

_____

_____

_____

THIS IS THE DAY
the Lord has made;
WE WILL REJOICE
and be glad in it

Psalm 118:24

This is the day which the Lord hath made; we will rejoice and be glad in it.
—Psalm 118:24

Lord, give me gratitude for this day, for each new day is a priceless opportunity to live, to laugh, and to love. Help me celebrate this day with all my heart, rejoicing in the sunrise and sunset, giving thanks for your constant presence, and cherishing the chance to work and play, to think and speak—knowing this: All simple pleasures are opportunities for praise. Thank you, Lord, for this day.

MY THOUGHTS

MY PRAYER REQUESTS

I'M GRATEFUL FOR

_____

_____

_____

_____

_____

_____

_____

_____

_____

_____

HOPE

*Let us hold fast the profession of our
faith without wavering, for he is
faithful that promised.*
–Hebrews 10:23

Lord, I know you are supremely faithful!
Today I ask you to restore hope to the
hopeless. Plant seeds of hope in hearts
that have lain fallow for so long. Send down
showers of hope on those struggling with
illness, persecution, or difficult relationships.
Your hope has the power to sustain us—even
when nothing seems the least bit hopeful.

MY THOUGHTS

MY PRAYER REQUESTS

MY HOPES

_____

_____

_____

_____

_____

_____

_____

_____

_____

_____

_____

Be of good courage, and he shall strengthen your heart, all ye that hope in the Lord.
—Psalm 31:24

Lord, let me be strong today, drawing my courage from my hope in you. Help me lean not on my own strength but on your limitless power. I know there is work to be done— burdens to be lifted, temptations to be resisted, and unkindness to be forgiven. Let my thoughts and actions be motivated by my hope in you.

MY THOUGHTS

_____

_____

_____

_____

_____

_____

_____

_____

_____

_____

_____

_____

MY PRAYER REQUESTS

_____

_____

_____

_____

_____

_____

_____

_____

_____

_____

_____

_____

MY HOPES

_____

_____

_____

_____

_____

_____

_____

_____

_____

_____

_____

_____

WE HAVE THIS *Hope* AS AN ANCHOR FOR THE *Soul*

*We might have a strong consolation,
who have fled for refuge to lay hold upon
the hope set before us: Which hope we
have as an anchor of the soul,
both sure and stedfast.*

—Hebrews 6:18–19

Hope is an anchor to the soul. When tossed and turned upon the waves of life, I will take refuge in you, O God. When the darkness descends upon my home, I will fear not, for I will place my faith in you, God. When a loved one is ill or hurt, I will remain steadfast, for I know that you will be right there among us.

MY THOUGHTS

MY PRAYER REQUESTS

_____

_____

_____

_____

_____

_____

_____

_____

_____

_____

_____

_____

_____

MY HOPES

_____

_____

_____

_____

_____

_____

_____

_____

_____

_____

_____

*Blessed is the man that trusteth in the Lord,
and whose hope the Lord is.*
—Jeremiah 17:7

Lord, maybe it's in the times I'm not sure that you are hearing my prayers that I learn to trust you the most. Eventually—in your time—I hear your answer. I know that all my hopes and dreams are safe in your hands. Even when the answer to a prayer is "no," I am comforted by the knowledge that you care about me and respond to my concerns in a way that will ultimately be for my good.

MY THOUGHTS

MY PRAYER REQUESTS

_____

_____

_____

_____

_____

_____

_____

_____

_____

_____

_____

_____

_____

MY HOPES

_____

_____

_____

_____

_____

_____

_____

_____

_____

_____

_____

FAITH

*For therein is the righteousness of God
revealed from faith to faith: as it is written,
The just shall live by faith.*
—Romans 1:17

Faith is more than a passive idea; it's a
principle that motivates our day-to-day
actions. We daily act upon things we believe
in, though we cannot yet see the end result.
We do things that are motivated by our faith
in things promised but not yet fulfilled.
We smile in the face of adversity.
We continue in prayer even when our prayers
seem to go unanswered. We stop saying,
"I can't" and start believing God can!
Step by step, we put our faith into action
and learn to "live by faith."

MY THOUGHTS

MY PRAYER REQUESTS

_____

_____

_____

_____

_____

_____

_____

_____

_____

_____

_____

_____

BOLSTER MY FAITH IN

_____

_____

_____

_____

_____

_____

_____

_____

_____

_____

_____

LET GO and LET GOD

Trust in the Lord with all thine heart; and lean not unto thine own understanding.
—Proverbs 3:5

Lord, sometimes I need to be reminded to have faith and "let go." Last night in bed I stared into the darkness, worrying about bills, my workload, my aging parents. My mind churned as I envisioned ways to exert control. It was only when I "let go" and turned my concerns over to you that I earned some measure of peace, and was able to sleep. Lord, thank you for your support as I navigate my busy days. May I have the faith to trust you over my own understanding.

MY THOUGHTS

MY PRAYER REQUESTS

_____

_____

_____

_____

_____

_____

_____

_____

_____

_____

_____

BOLSTER MY FAITH IN

_____

_____

_____

_____

_____

_____

_____

_____

_____

_____

_____

_____

_____

WALK BY faith NOT BY sight

The Lord, he it is that doth go before thee;
he will be with thee, he will not fail thee,
neither forsake thee: fear not,
neither be dismayed.
—Deuteronomy 31:8

Lord, give me the faith to take the next step,
even when I don't know what lies ahead.
Give me the assurance that even if I
stumble and fall, you'll pick me up and
put me back on the path. And give me
the confidence that, even if I lose faith,
you will never lose me.

MY THOUGHTS

MY PRAYER REQUESTS

_____

_____

_____

_____

_____

_____

_____

_____

_____

_____

_____

_____

BOLSTER MY FAITH IN

_____

_____

_____

_____

_____

_____

_____

_____

_____

_____

_____

BE STRONG & COURAGEOUS

JOSHUA 1:6

*Be strong and of a good courage; be
not afraid, neither be thou dismayed:
for the Lord thy God is with thee
whithersoever thou goest.*
—Joshua 1:9

Seeking courage, Heavenly Father, I bundle
my fears and place them in your hands.
Such shadowy terrors wither to nothing in
your grasp. I know I have nothing to fear
when you are the one caring for me, Father.
And yet, I do fear, despite your faithfulness,
assurances, and promises. Please liberate me
from these lapses of trust. Free me to stand
fearlessly, supported by faith and hope, in
the center of your great love for me.

MY THOUGHTS

MY PRAYER REQUESTS

_____

_____

_____

_____

_____

_____

_____

_____

_____

_____

_____

_____

_____

BOLSTER MY FAITH IN

_____

_____

_____

_____

_____

_____

_____

_____

_____

_____

LOVE

Neither death, nor life, nor angels, nor principalities, nor powers, nor things present, nor things to come, nor height, nor depth, nor any other creature, shall be able to separate us from the love of God.

—Romans 8:38–39

Lord God, there is no mountain high enough, no valley deep enough, no obstacle large enough to separate your love from me. Your love is wider than my worries, longer than my loneliness, stronger than my sorrows, and deeper than my doubts. Your love never fails and never disappoints. Help me love those I encounter today as graciously as you love me.

MY THOUGHTS

_____

_____

_____

_____

_____

_____

_____

_____

_____

_____

_____

_____

_____

MY PRAYER REQUESTS

WHAT'S ON MY HEART

_____

_____

_____

_____

_____

_____

_____

_____

_____

_____

_____

You shall love the Lord your God with all your heart and with all your soul and with all your strength

Deuteronomy 6:5

Thou shalt love the Lord thy God with all thy heart, and with all thy soul, and with all thy mind. This is the first and great commandment.
—Matthew 22:37–38

Lord, I truly want to love you with all my heart, soul, and mind as you commanded— so why do I have such a hard time doing it? At times my heart is fully engaged in loving you, but my soul feels weary and my mind goes wandering down another path. Unite my heart, soul, and mind, Lord, so I can stay wholly focused on loving you.

MY THOUGHTS

MY PRAYER REQUESTS

WHAT'S ON MY HEART

_____

_____

_____

_____

_____

_____

_____

_____

_____

_____

_____

THE FRUIT OF THE SPIRIT IS LOVE, JOY, PEACE, LONGSUFFERING KINDNESS, GOODNESS FAITHFULNESS GENTLENESS SELF-CONTROL GAL. 5:22

The fruit of the Spirit is love, joy, peace, longsuffering, gentleness, goodness, faith, meekness, temperance: against such there is no law.
—Galatians 5:22–23

Lord, how I pray that your love is evident in me today! I want to follow you closely and help draw others to you as well. I know that if those with whom I come in contact see love, joy, peace, patience, kindness, goodness, faithfulness, gentleness, and self-control in me, they may find you as well. Direct my steps as I follow you, Lord. Let me seek your Spirit and practice these virtues.

MY THOUGHTS

_____

_____

_____

_____

_____

_____

_____

_____

_____

_____

_____

_____

_____

_____

MY PRAYER REQUESTS

_____

_____

_____

_____

_____

_____

_____

_____

_____

_____

_____

_____

WHAT'S ON MY HEART

_____

_____

_____

_____

_____

_____

_____

_____

_____

_____

_____

Love your neighbor as yourself

MARK 12:31

Thou shalt love thy neighbour as thyself.
—Mark 12:31

O God, your love is so great. But sometimes
I'm not sure that I can love as you do or
even love others in a way that will please
you. Teach me how to really love my family,
friends, neighbors, and even strangers. It's so
easy to get tangled up in my own isolating
concerns. God, prod me to turn my love
outward. I trust in the power of your love
to make me into a far more loving
person than I am today. Amen.

MY THOUGHTS

MY PRAYER REQUESTS

WHAT'S ON MY HEART

_____

_____

_____

_____

_____

_____

_____

_____

_____

_____

_____

GUIDANCE

A man's heart deviseth his way: but the Lord directeth his steps.

—Proverbs 16:9

Dear Lord, all my plans have been tossed in the air like so many grains of rice, never to be gathered or ordered again. I thought I had it all figured out, but now I'm unsure. Remind me that the only sure thing is you. When I devise plans without consulting you, I always run into problems. Direct my steps, Lord. Help me find the right path—not the path of my choosing but the path you have planned for me.

MY THOUGHTS

MY PRAYER REQUESTS

_____

_____

_____

_____

_____

_____

_____

_____

_____

_____

_____

_____

_____

GUIDE ME

_____

_____

_____

_____

_____

_____

_____

_____

_____

_____

_____

PSALM 37:5

COMMIT
your way

TO THE LORD

TRUST *also* IN HIM

&

HE SHALL

BRING IT
to pass

Commit thy way unto the Lord; trust also in him; and he shall bring it to pass.
—Psalm 37:5

Lord, this is one of those days when I really don't know which way to turn. I've lost my sense of direction and need you to lead me back to familiar ground. Please guide me, Lord, through this unfamiliar territory. Send the signs I need to follow. For I know that it is only when you are leading me that I am moving in the right direction. I put my trust in you.

MY THOUGHTS

MY PRAYER REQUESTS

_____

_____

_____

_____

_____

_____

_____

_____

_____

_____

_____

_____

GUIDE ME

_____

_____

_____

_____

_____

_____

_____

_____

_____

_____

_____

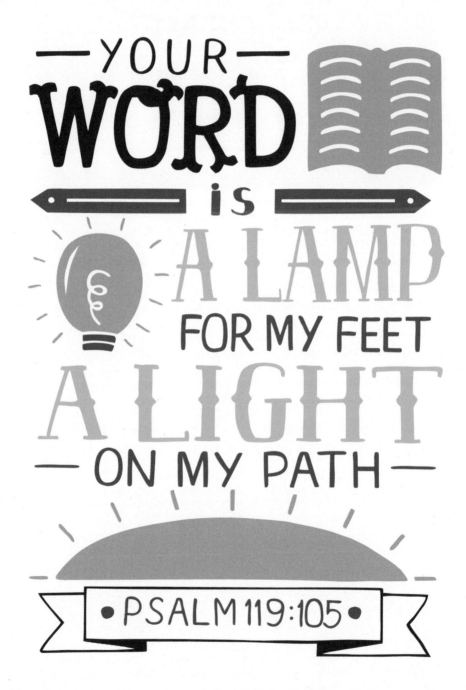

YOUR WORD is A LAMP FOR MY FEET A LIGHT ON MY PATH

• PSALM 119:105 •

*For thou art my lamp, O Lord: and
the Lord will lighten my darkness.*
—2 Samuel 22:29

When I leave you behind and try to go about
my day without your guidance, Lord, it's like
groping around in the dark. I stub my heart
on relationship issues. I trip over my ego. I
fall down the steps of my foolish choices.
How much better to seek the light of your
presence first thing and enjoy the benefit of
having you illuminate each step of my day!

MY THOUGHTS

_____

_____

_____

_____

_____

_____

_____

_____

_____

_____

_____

_____

_____

MY PRAYER REQUESTS

_____

_____

_____

_____

_____

_____

_____

_____

_____

_____

_____

_____

_____

GUIDE ME

_____

_____

_____

_____

_____

_____

_____

_____

_____

_____

_____

I AM THE GOOD- SHEPHERD

I am the good shepherd, and know my sheep, and am known of mine.
—John 10:14

Your Word says that a flock of sheep knows its own shepherd's voice and won't respond to the voice of a different shepherd. It's true of my relationship with you, too, Lord. I know your voice. I know when you're speaking to my heart, and I know when I'm being coaxed by "other voices"—wrong desires, worldly values, anxiety, pride, and the like. Thanks for helping me see the difference. Coax me to follow the sound of your voice today and always.

MY THOUGHTS

MY PRAYER REQUESTS

_____

_____

_____

_____

_____

_____

_____

_____

_____

_____

_____

_____

_____

GUIDE ME

_____

_____

_____

_____

_____

_____

_____

_____

_____

_____

PEACE

The peace of God, which passeth all understanding, shall keep your hearts and minds through Christ Jesus.
—Philippians 4:7

Dear God, I long to feel the peace you bring, the peace that passes all understanding. These trying times leave me anxious and worried for my future. Fill my entire being with the light of your love, your grace, and your everlasting mercy. Be the soft place that I might fall upon to find the rest and renewal I seek. Amen.

MY THOUGHTS

MY PRAYER REQUESTS

_____

_____

_____

_____

_____

_____

_____

_____

_____

_____

_____

_____

BRING PEACE TO

_____

_____

_____

_____

_____

_____

_____

_____

_____

_____

_____

BLESSED
are the
PEACEMAKERS
for they
will be called
SONS OF GOD

Blessed are the peacemakers: for they shall be called the children of God.
—Matthew 5:9

Lord, you are the greatest of all peacemakers. Show me how to follow your example today. Bless me with a peacemaker's kind heart and a builder's sturdy hand, Lord, for these are mean-spirited, litigious times when we tear down with words and weapons first and ask questions later. Help me take every opportunity to compliment, praise, and applaud as I rebuild peace.

MY THOUGHTS

MY PRAYER REQUESTS

BRING PEACE TO

_____

_____

_____

_____

_____

_____

_____

_____

_____

_____

_____

_____

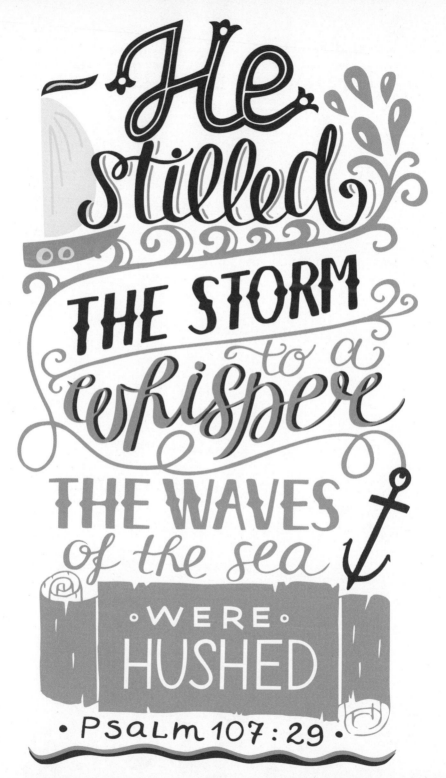

He stilled THE STORM to a whisper THE WAVES of the sea WERE HUSHED

• Psalm 107:29 •

He maketh the storm a calm, so that the waves thereof are still. Then are they glad because they be quiet; so he bringeth them unto their desired haven.

—Psalm 107:29–30

You calmed the stormy waters, Lord, and quieted the thunderous skies. You who brought peace in the midst of the storm are the only one who can bring peace to our world today. How much anger we see raging around us, Lord. And the conflicts are not limited to wars in distant lands. Rather they rage in our hearts and minds. Be the source of peace in every gathering storm, Lord.

MY THOUGHTS

MY PRAYER REQUESTS

BRING PEACE TO

_____

_____

_____

_____

_____

_____

_____

_____

_____

_____

GRACE

Having then gifts differing according to the grace that is given to us.
—Romans 12:6

Creator God, how wise of you to make us all intriguingly different and to send a variety of gifts into the world through us. How boring it would be if everyone in one church had the gift of preaching, but no one had the gift of hospitality. How ineffective your church would be if no one had the gifts of serving or mercy as well. But by your grace we have different gifts. Thank you for them all, God.

MY THOUGHTS

MY PRAYER REQUESTS

_____

_____

_____

_____

_____

_____

_____

_____

_____

_____

_____

_____

_____

GRANT ME GRACE

_____

_____

_____

_____

_____

_____

_____

_____

_____

_____

_____

_____

_____

BY GRACE
through
FAITH
in Christ

For by grace are ye saved through faith; and that not of yourselves: it is the gift of God: Not of works, lest any man should boast.
—Ephesians 2:8–9

Lord, I am grateful that you don't have a list of criteria for being eligible for salvation. What insecurity that would create in me! I feel blessed that I don't need to resort to servile fear or self-important boasting when it comes to my standing with you.
Your salvation is a gift available to all and secured by your merits, not mine. It is received only by grace through faith in you.

MY THOUGHTS

MY PRAYER REQUESTS

_____

_____

_____

_____

_____

_____

_____

_____

_____

_____

_____

_____

GRANT ME GRACE

_____

_____

_____

_____

_____

_____

_____

_____

_____

_____

_____

_____

My Grace is sufficient for you

My grace is sufficient for thee: for my strength is made perfect in weakness. Most gladly therefore will I rather glory in my infirmities, that the power of Christ may rest upon me.
—2 Corinthians 12:9

Gracious God, of all your gifts, grace may be the most glorious! With your unmerited favor falling upon me, I can survive almost anything. In times of plenty or of want, your grace is sufficient. When I feel so exhausted I don't know how I'll get through the morning, let alone the day, your grace is sufficient. And when serious illness strikes, your grace is sufficient. Thank you, God, for your marvelous gift of grace.

MY THOUGHTS

MY PRAYER REQUESTS

_____

_____

_____

_____

_____

_____

_____

_____

_____

_____

_____

_____

_____

GRANT ME GRACE

_____

_____

_____

_____

_____

_____

_____

_____

_____

_____

_____

_____

_____

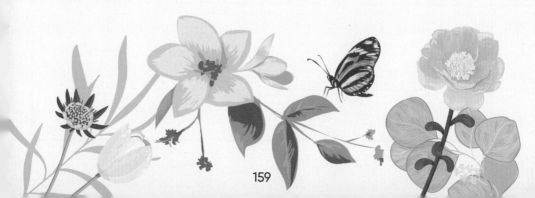